KNAPP, B.
Mountains

SCHOOLS

Kingston upon Hull City Libraries
WITHDRAWN FROM STOCK

FOR SALE

PROJECT

ALS No. B278293544

This item should be returned on or before the last date stamped above. If not in demand it may be renewed for a further period by personal application, by telephone, or in writing. The author, title, above number and date due back should be quoted.

LS/3

MOUNTAINS

SIMON & SCHUSTER
YOUNG BOOKS

First Published in 1992 by
Simon & Schuster Young Books
Campus 400
Maylands Avenue
Hemel Hempstead
Hertfordshire HP2 7EZ
England

Copyright © 1992 by Simon & Schuster Young Books

British Library Cataloguing in Publication Data

Knapp, Brian
  Mountains (Caring for environments)
  1. Mountains – Juvenile literature
  I. Title   II. Series
  551.4

ISBN 0-7500-1038-X

Printed and bound in Hong Kong

All rights reserved. No part of this publication may be reproduced, stored in a retrieval system, or transmitted in any form or by any means otherwise, without prior permission in writing of the publisher, nor be otherwise circulated in any form of binding or cover other than that in which it is published and without a similar condition including this condition being imposed on the subsequent purchaser.

Author Dr. Brian Knapp
Art Director Duncan McCrae
Illustrator Mark Franklin
Designed and produced by
EARTHSCAPE EDITIONS,
86 Peppard Road,
Sonning Common, Reading,
Berkshire, RG4 9RP, UK

Picture credits

t=top b=bottom l=left r=right

All photographs from the Earthscape Editions photographic library except the following:
Brian Hoskins 29; Huchison Library 27, 43; USGS 20; ZEFA – front cover

CONTENTS

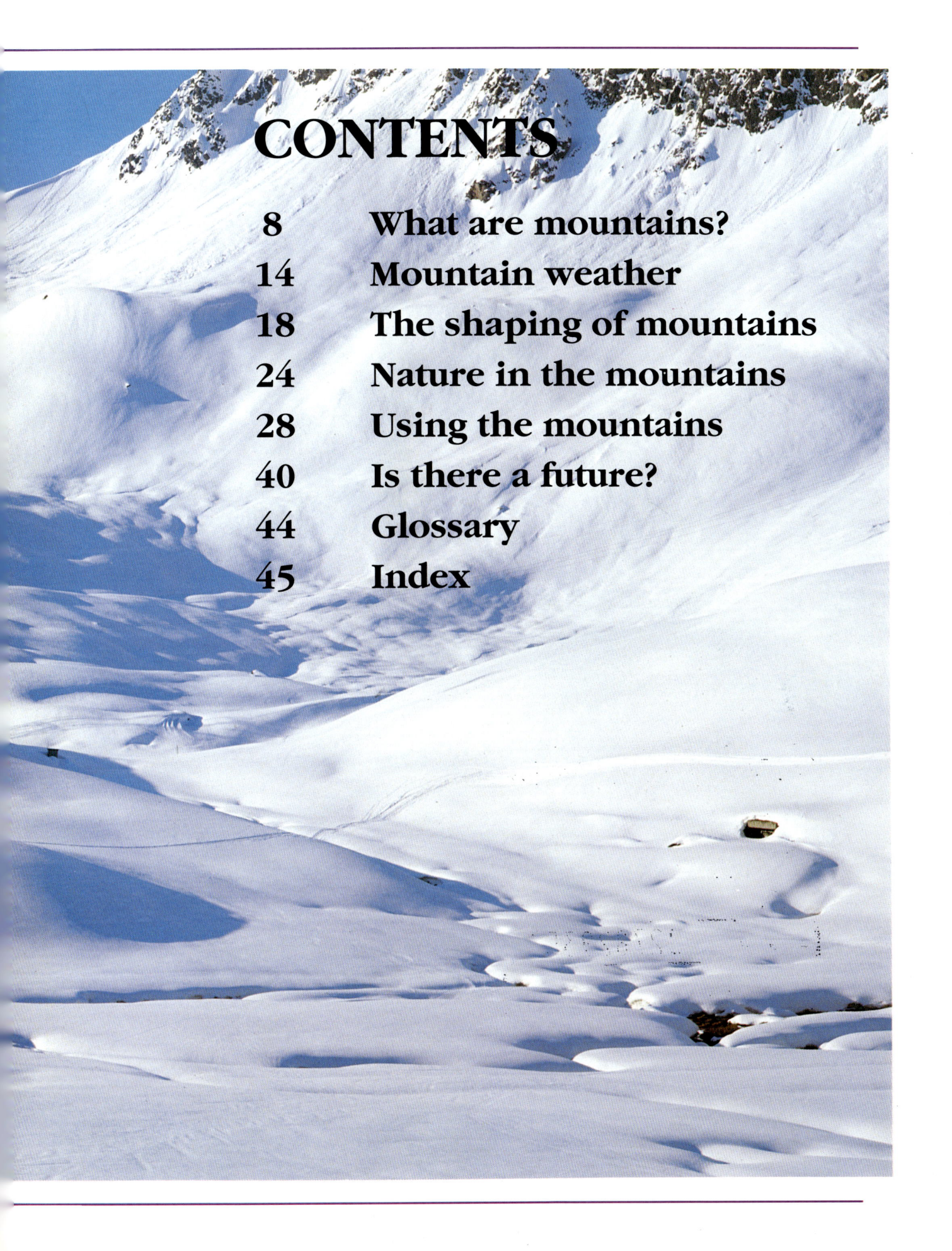

8	What are mountains?
14	Mountain weather
18	The shaping of mountains
24	Nature in the mountains
28	Using the mountains
40	Is there a future?
44	Glossary
45	Index

1: WHAT ARE MOUNTAINS?

In January 1953, after a trial of strength and endurance that had lasted many months and required a small army of supporters, Edmund Hillary of New Zealand and Tenzing Norgay of Nepal staggered the last few gruelling paces to the top of the highest peak in the world. They had fought cold, glaciers and lack of oxygen to get to the summit of Mount Everest, the world's highest mountain.

__High, rugged mountains have always seemed the ultimate challenge__ to some people. But mountains are also home to many and the place for holidays to huge numbers more.
  Because so many people compete for the use of the mountain environment, everyone must find ways to use the mountains carefully for, although they are made of tough rock, they are also areas with environments that are extremely fragile.

Many farms in mountainous areas lie abandoned. *Their owners have long since migrated to the valleys in search of an easier way of life. Here the land which once saw controlled grazing is now being changed to forest.*

The limited number of routes *through a mountainous region was used to advantage by landowners in the past. They built castles to defend their territories or to charge tolls for using the routes. Although tolls are now uncommon, the routes remain crucial to people who use the mountains.*

Mountains are places of high relief which stand out from the surrounding plains. There is no special height that determines whether a piece of land should be called a mountain or not. The valley bottoms between the Swiss mountains, for example, are further above sea level than the tops of the highest British 'mountains'.

Mountains are special places because of the profound influence they have on the lives of people. They are hostile places where the weather makes living difficult. They can act as a barrier, keeping people on one side isolated from their neighbours on the other side. They can also be a bond – the hard life giving all mountain people something in common.

Although the mountains have traditionally been the homes of farmers, there have been many other people wanting to make use of the land. For some it has just been for the challenge of getting to the top of a peak, for others the opportunity to get spectacular views, and for yet others the promise of untold riches of gold and silver buried in the mountains' rocks.

WHAT ARE MOUNTAINS?

Mountains have so inspired people in some countries such as Tibet, Japan and Indonesia, that they worship their gods from peaks, or even revere the mountains themselves.

This Balinese volcano *has long had a religious importance and many temples have been built on its lower flanks. The periodic eruptions have simply added to the sense of awe that people have felt for their mountain.*

In the past people had obvious practical needs for securing the mountain peaks. They are good places for defence, and you can see the enemy coming from far afield. Today, by contrast, the mountains are heavily visited by tourists: in winter mainly for ski sports, in summer for walking and sightseeing. Mountains now need protecting from people who may, through weight of numbers, destroy the very things they have come to see.

WHAT ARE MOUNTAINS?

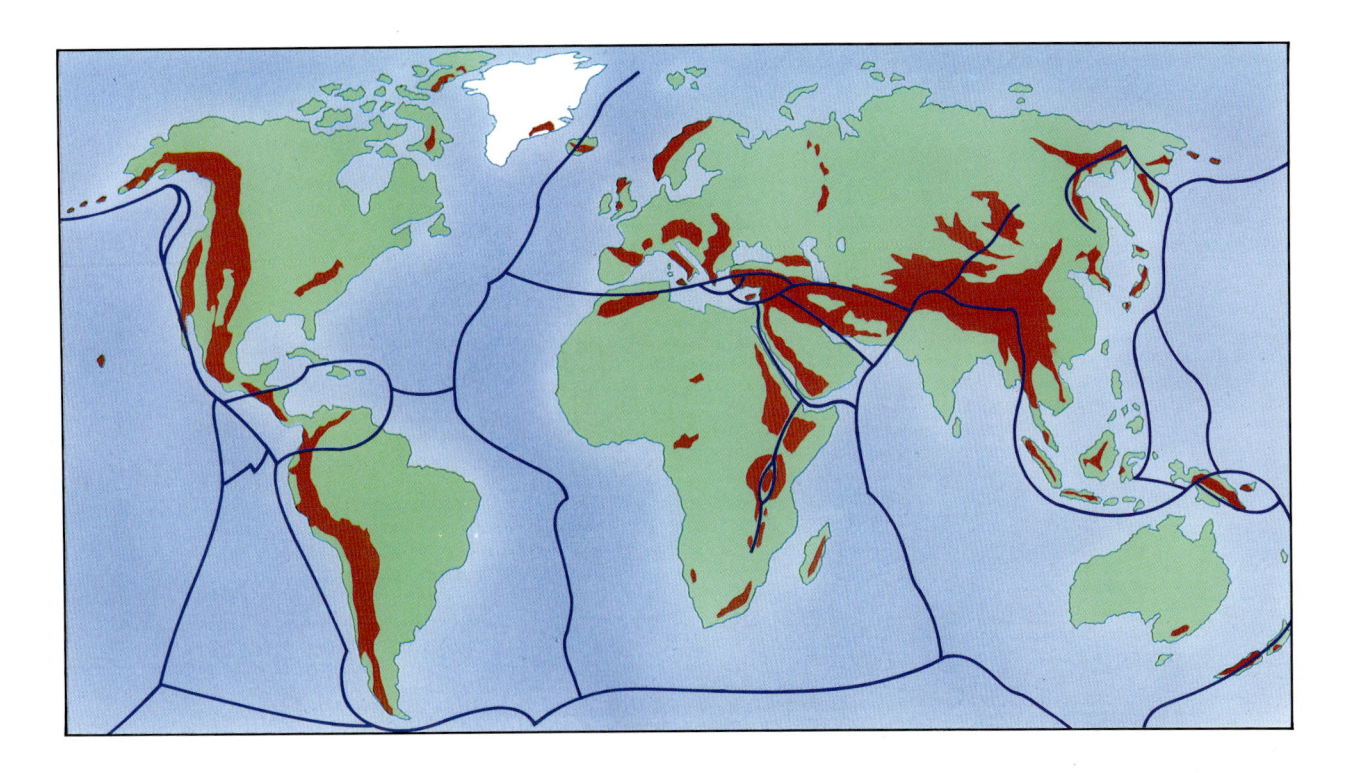

The world's continental mountains *are formed from folded rocks and mainly grouped into long chains; the ocean mountains are all individual volcanoes. All mountains are associated with movements of the Earth's crust.*

Seeing detail

For many reasons mountains have had a strong influence on the lives of people. But all too often the mountains are seen either too close – rock by rock as they climb a mountain face – or from too far away, as they gaze on beautiful summits from nearby plains. As a result the way mountains form and change, and the impact people can have on these environments is not seen. What is needed is to look at mountains in another way: to see them from the viewpoint of the natural world – how they form part of a wild landscape that is home to an amazing variety of plants and animals, and also as a place that is fragile and one that can easily be destroyed.

When you look at mountains in this way the first thing you notice is that they are not all the same. Even Mount Everest is not what it at first seems – the world's highest peak. As it happens this title really belongs to one of the Hawaiian islands. Its volcanic peak appears to rise very modestly from the sea. However, the island is just the mere tip of a giant mountain that rises more than 24 kilometres from the ocean bed.

In fact, many types of mountain have been formed during the development of the planet and some are still being actively formed. Many mountains, especially those in the Pacific Ocean, are single volcanoes. Others, like the Himalayas of Asia and the Andes and Rockies of the Americas, have formed from sheets of folded rocks that once lay under the sea. Each type of mountain develops its own patterns of rock and soil, and supports wildlife in a unique way.

WHAT ARE MOUNTAINS? 11

Skiing has done more than any other activity *to cause changes in the mountains. Skiing is now a sport that is available to millions of people each year, yet few believe that skiing on snow can be any threat to a mountain environment.*

The mountains influence the weather and provide homes for a multitude of plants and animals. But as the mountains are high, the weather is harsh, and their wildlife is slow to grow and slow to change. In the past people have learned that they must inhabit these regions with care. Through long experience they have learned how to work with mountain environments, and they have learned how to remain in some kind of peaceful equilibrium with the natural world. But in the twentieth century technology can change the pace of mountain use very rapidly. In Utah, USA, machines have scraped out the world's largest hole as they sift the rocks for copper; in the Andes, whole tracts of mountains are scarred and disfigured by the search for minerals. In the Alps the huge numbers of skiers have been catered for by building new tourist resorts and motorways. At the same time traditional ways of farming have become uneconomic because their small scale methods on difficult land cannot produce food as cheaply as the mechanized farmers of the lowland. As a result, mountains are often places from which the traditional people are retreating.

Without care, mountain environments could easily become unrecognizable in just a few decades. But the problem of caring for these environments is so complicated that it needs to be looked at in a number of stages. That is why the first section of this book looks at how the weather changes from mountain summit to base and from windward side to leeward side, and how plants and animals have become adapted to the mountain environment. The second

WHAT ARE MOUNTAINS?

part examines the way mountains are formed and then shaped by erosion. The third part shows how people have used the mountains in the past and some of the ways they plan to use them. Finally, we shall see what future there is for mountains, and the best way to treat the environments for their long-term survival.

While the high summits remain inaccessible *to all but a few, and are therefore relatively free from harm, the lower and more accessible summits that are readily reached by road can easily become overused and subject to erosion. In many countries the main long distance mountain paths have had to be surfaced, in order to take the strain.*

In many parts of the developing world, *mountains are still negotiated using age-old paths. Such primitive routes restrict the numbers who can make use of the land. However, as developing countries begin to open up their mountains to tourists and build new roads, the pressure on the environment is sure to increase rapidly.*

WHAT ARE MOUNTAINS? 13

2: MOUNTAIN WEATHER

Mountain weather is unpredictable and often wild. A sunny day can suddenly change into a blizzard; a clearly seen peak can swiftly disappear in the mist.

Anyone who lives in or visits mountains must be aware of the special weather patterns, for they often play a major role in determining the nature of the natural environment, how people traditionally use the land, and the dangers that may befall strangers.

Fitful mists hide these Swiss mountain tops. Changes and unpredictability are the keynotes of mountain weather.

High, clear and cold

In the simplest terms, mountain weather changes towards the summit because higher up in the atmosphere the air gets steadily colder and thinner. Cold air can hold less moisture than warm, so as air is forced up a mountain front it releases the surplus as rain or snow – giving the high precipitation amounts for which many mountains are renowned. Surprisingly perhaps, the very highest peaks are true deserts. At these heights nearly all the moisture has been shed, the sun shines nearly all year and the snow that falls rarely melts.

People who climb mountains are often aware of the lack of oxygen in the air because, as they climb higher, breathing becomes more difficult, and in extreme cases they can get altitude sickness. Over the centuries, all animals, and the traditional people who live in high altitude regions, have become adapted to deal with this problem.

Two-faced mountains

In large measure mountains create their own weather. They block the path of the winds that blow over the Earth, forcing them to pile up on what is referred to as the windward side of the mountain, then rush over the summits before escaping to the leeward side. In the process air is first squeezed and cooled, making cloud and driving winds, then expanded and warmed, giving clear rain-free skies. It is a dramatic change which can mean that the weather on one side of a mountain is also totally different from that on the other side, just a few kilometres away.

MOUNTAIN WEATHER

Moisture
shed as rain

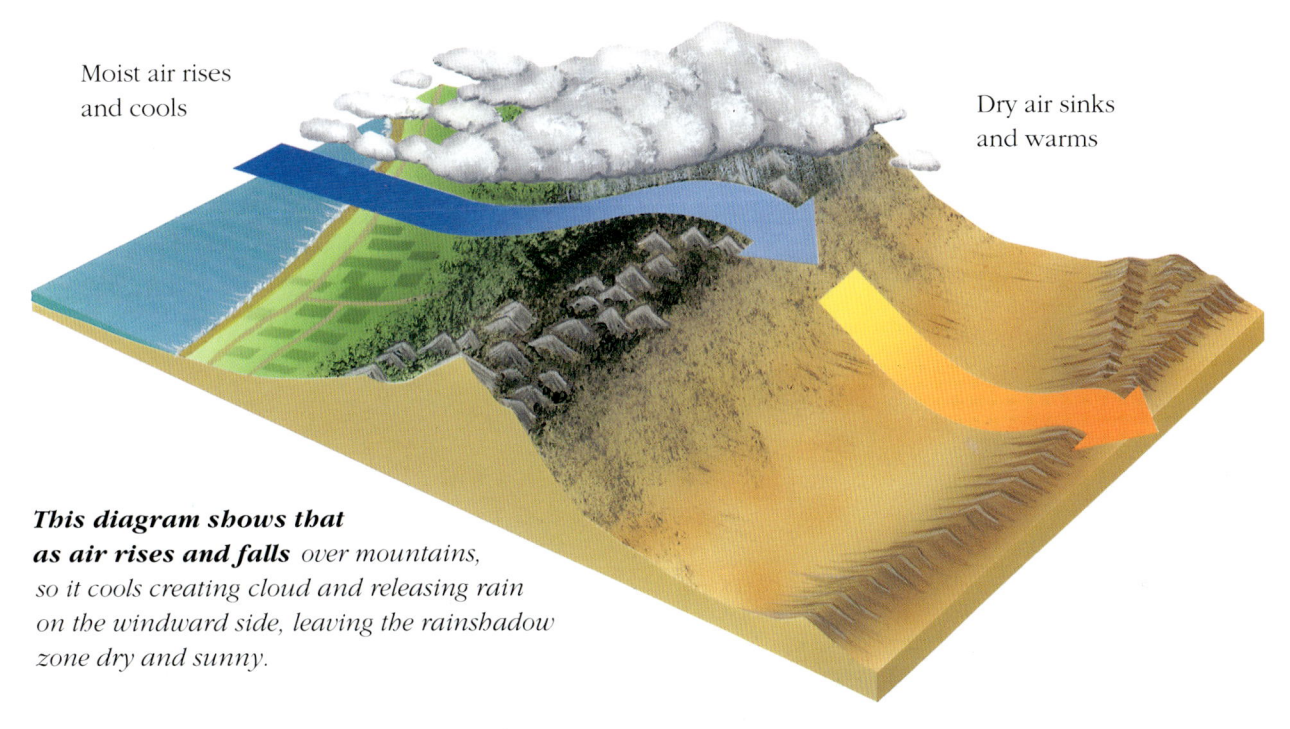

Moist air rises
and cools

Dry air sinks
and warms

This diagram shows that as air rises and falls over mountains, so it cools creating cloud and releasing rain on the windward side, leaving the rainshadow zone dry and sunny.

The lee side of a mountain range can be very dry. This is reflected in the sparse vegetation.

MOUNTAIN WEATHER

Early morning leaves the lower valley slopes cold and sunless. *Traditionally people have chosen the sites for their homes with care, preferring to build them clear of the valley bottoms and on the side of the valley that faces the early morning sun.*

The windward faces suffer the bulk of the cloud and receive the bulk of the rain. This relief rain causes windward slopes to be frequently shrouded in thick sheets of cloud. But as the air finally rides over the mountain crests and begins to sink down the lee side, the rain ceases and the clouds quickly evaporate, often leaving the lee side bathed in sunshine. But sunny weather has its penalties and the leeward sides of mountains can often be very short of water. In areas with less impressive mountains such as Britain, the rainfall on the windward slopes may be four or five times that of the **rainshadow** region. The highest mountains – the Himalayas – have the world's highest rainfall on one side (at Cherrapunji, India, 1800 centimetres) and nearly the lowest (Tibet, 20 centimetres) on the other.

When there are several mountain ranges separated by wide open valleys, as is the case with the Sierra Nevada of California, in the United States, the ocean winds blow onshore and are forced up each mountain range in turn. They then sink into the next valley. The effect is to make the air experience a flow more like a roller coaster, and on each upward movement more precious moisture is lost until, on the final fall into Death Valley, there is almost no moisture left and the valley receives an average of less than 2 centimetres of rain a year.

Mountain and valley winds

High mountains induce a wide range of local weather effects, including some ferocious winds and penetrating frosts. These, more than anything, control the successful growing season for mountain plants.

MOUNTAIN WEATHER

Smoke from a bonfire in a mountain valley *shows clearly how the valley and mountain winds work. Instead of rising, the smoke meets an invisible ceiling of sinking air which holds the smoke close to the ground. Of course, any factory chimney smoke and vehicle exhaust fumes will be trapped in valleys in the same way. Such pollution may cause harm to the natural vegetation.*

On days when the sky is clear, quite gentle winds are set up simply by the way the sun's rays heat the valley sides. In the early morning the tops of the mountains may be bathed in sunshine while the valleys are deep in shadow.

The warmed air on the upper slopes rises, drawing the cold air upwards from the valleys and causing a mountain wind.

By late afternoon, the sun is setting, and the balance of heating and cooling changes. The sheltered valleys hold the heat for longer, while the open, upper slopes cool quickly. The air resting on the upper slopes is thus chilled, becomes heavy, and starts to roll down into the valley bottoms. This valley wind is cold and can swiftly bring frost to the valley and shroud the lower slopes in fog that takes a long time to lift.

3: THE SHAPING OF MOUNTAINS

Mountains take many millions of years to form and eventually wear down to plains. The Alps, Himalayas, Rockies and Andes are all over 100 million years old; the Appalachians of North America, the mountains of north and west Britain and the mountains of Scandinavia are far older. Yet despite their age, mountains are constantly changing under the effects of snow, ice, rain and sun. They can also suffer catastrophic changes at the hands of people.

The secrets of mountain ranges

At first sight mountains may seem much the same, but in reality there are many types of mountains. The Alps, Rockies and Himalayas, for example, form long narrow and well defined belts over the Earth's surface. In recent years geologists have realized that these mountains are the result of collisions between huge pieces of the Earth's **crust** – called **plates** – as they drift slowly across the surface of the globe, driven by forces deep within the Earth. This is known as continental drift.

Geologists now understand that as two plates collide they crush up the ocean floor that once separated them, thrusting **sediments** that were once formed deep under the oceans, many kilometres above sea level. Even the rocks that make the mighty heights of Mount Everest were once in the depths of the ocean.

But at the same time as the ocean floor is buckled, scraped, squeezed and thrust into a high **fold mountain** range, so more rock is pushed down into the crust to balance it. In a sense the mountains we see today are like the tips of an iceberg. They only hint at the real size of the mountains. Geologists call the buried regions of the mountains 'roots' and they are the key to the survival of the mountains over hundreds of millions of years. Indeed, the mountain ranges 'float' on the 'liquid' rocks below the Earth's surface. As a result, as the forces of erosion wear away the mountains,

Parallel mountain ranges, such as these in northern Iraq, were formed as continents collided. The rugged form is due to the action of frost and glaciers.

THE SHAPING OF MOUNTAINS

Island arc   Mid ocean mountain range   Fold mountain range with volcanoes

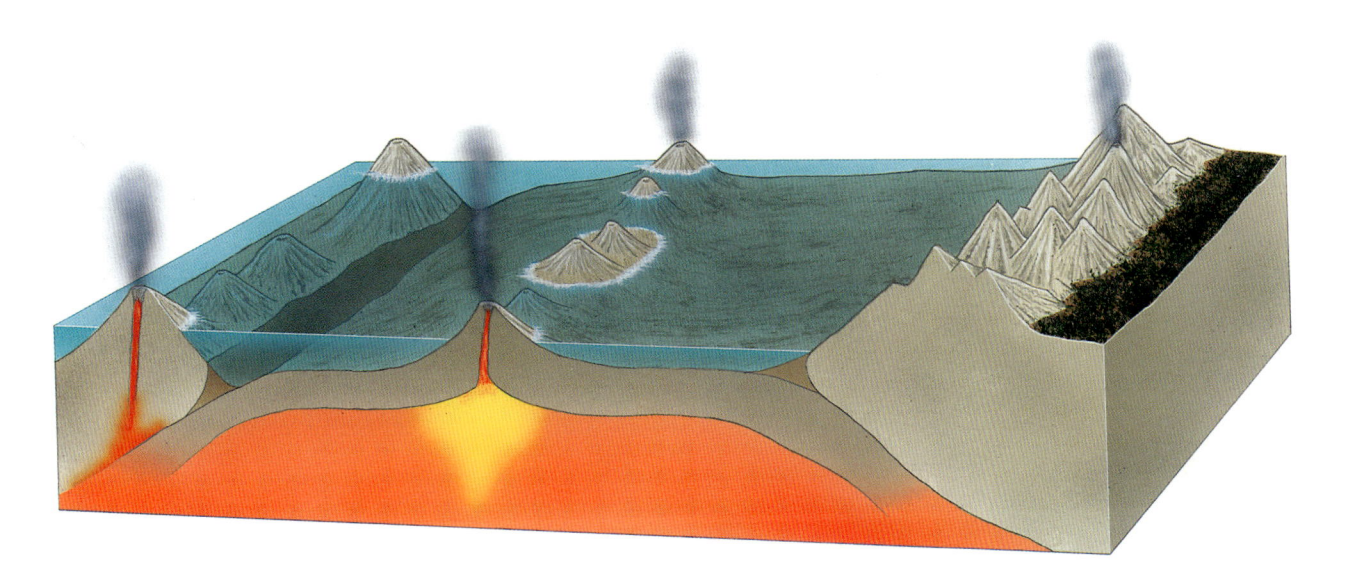

so the roots rise to compensate for the loss in overlying weight. This is the secret of the mountains' long survival.

Ranges in the oceans

As continents drift into each other as a result of the plates moving, so elsewhere they must drift apart, causing profound fractures that go down to the Earth's **mantle**. In the upper regions of the mantle some of the rock is still molten and it rises up the fractures, periodically spilling over the land or the ocean floors in huge sheets of lava. Eventually these accumulating lavas can form the world's biggest and broadest mountains such as those that run down the middle of the Atlantic Ocean.

Many of these mountain chains are hidden by the waters of the oceans.

***Mountains form in many parts of the Earth**, but they are all linked to the way plates drift over the surface. This diagram shows how splitting in the mid oceans allows volcanic mountains to form, while collisions at the edges may form either arcs of volcanic mountains or fold mountain ranges.*

Unlike the fold mountains they are young and simple, not old and complex. Also they are protected from erosion by being submerged under the sea.

Island arcs

There is one further group of mountains that are like neither land nor ocean mountains. They form the backbones of many of the world's island chains, making long arc-shaped patterns especially around the rim of the Pacific Ocean.

THE SHAPING OF MOUNTAINS

Island arcs, such as those of Indonesia or Japan, form as the ocean crust collides with the land. The ocean crust is then pushed below the land crust, scraping rock against rock and causing frequent earthquakes and sending huge plumes of lava to the surface as volcanic mountains.

All the mountains in Indonesia *are parts of island arcs with active volcanoes. Each volcano weathers to produce very fertile soils.*

This volcanic eruption *is happening on the Pacific island of Hawaii. The runny lava is basalt.*

Island volcanoes are new rock and they make new land. How well they survive erosion depends entirely on how new lava and ash is able to keep pace with the destruction caused by weathering.

Rocks that spell success or failure

To understand the mountain environment you need to know not only that there are different types of mountains, but also that they are made up of many different sorts of rocks, for example, limestone, sandstone and granite. It is the resistance of the rocks that determines how well they will stand up to erosion. However, the chemistry of the rocks will affect the fertility of a soil, how much mistreatment it will stand, and how quickly abused soil can recover.

The most fertile rocks are usually black in colour. This is the colour of lava in the oceans and in the island arcs. It contains a wealth of minerals that are good nutrients for plants. In tropical lands, where warmth and rainfall weather the rocks quickly, the soils on volcanoes are among the most

THE SHAPING OF MOUNTAINS

fertile in the world, making it desirable farmland. It is also one reason why so many people are in danger from volcanic eruptions.

The forbidding landscape of fold mountain valleys *is in part due to the tough rocks that weather into infertile soils. Heavy rainfall quickly removes most of the nutrients making the soils yet poorer. This is the reason many mountain landscapes cannot be farmed intensively.*

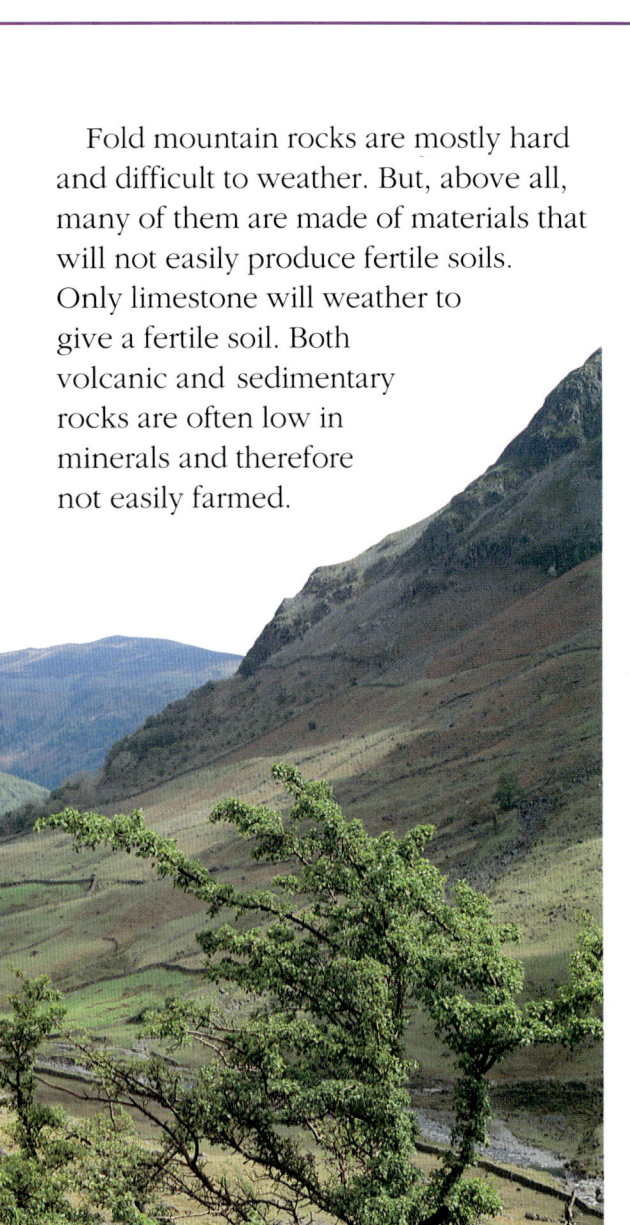

Fold mountain rocks are mostly hard and difficult to weather. But, above all, many of them are made of materials that will not easily produce fertile soils. Only limestone will weather to give a fertile soil. Both volcanic and sedimentary rocks are often low in minerals and therefore not easily farmed.

THE SHAPING OF MOUNTAINS

The glacier in the picture on the left spills out of a small valley left high above the floor of the main glacial trough. When the ice finally retreats thee tributary valleys will be left hanging far above the main valley floor. Waterfalls are common in such positions, as the picture below shows.

Where glaciers ranged

Many mountains still have glaciers that flow in deep valleys; in the past they were much larger and more powerful. The grinding, tearing action of glaciers in the last **Ice Age** was responsible both for the deep mountain valleys and the passes that allow people to cross from one valley to the next.

Glacial action begins when powdery snow compacts into ice. Ice is both heavy and mobile, and it can flow over rocks, down valleys, and even uphill.

As a glacier moves along a valley floor, the basal ice continually sticks to the rock and is then pushed on by the weight of ice up-slope. The tearing power of ice in these circumstances is enormous and huge pieces of rock can be wrenched clear of the bed and stuck to the base of the ice.

Glacial tearing – called quarrying – provides material that the ice base uses rather like the sand stuck to the surface of sandpaper. As the rock debris is pushed forwards, so it scrapes against the valley floor, grinding the surface into rock flour and destroying itself in the process.

THE SHAPING OF MOUNTAINS

But as each boulder gets ground away, another is torn from the rock bed and used for further scraping.

No time for change

The scouring and plucking effects of glaciers in mountains made powerful changes to the river valleys that preceded them. Where once there had been steep sided valleys with interlocking spurs and narrow flood plains, so glaciation left deeper, far wider valleys with no spurs at all.

It is just over 10 000 years ago since the ice covered nearly a third of the Earth. Today glaciers have retreated to the highest valleys and areas near the poles. But there has been little time for major alterations to the valley shapes left by glaciation. In the main, frost shattering has been the most active process on the valley sides, working on

Frost is the main agent of rock breakdown in mountain regions. Most frost cracking occurs in the spring and autumn when the air temperature hovers around freezing. Under these conditions snow may melt and flow into cracks in the rock during the day, only to freeze at night, expanding and breaking off flakes of rock in the process. It is frost shattering that has given this landscape its particularly jagged profile.

all the exposed rock faces, throwing down showers of rock fragments at each thaw which go to build the huge piles of debris called **screes**.

Rivers cut slowly and few have changed the glacial valley floor. Many floors are still covered by thick layers of debris (known as ground moraine or till) that were dropped by the glaciers as they melted away. Many rivers still fall from tributary valleys in spectacular cascades and waterfalls, while uneven valley floors are still filled with lakes.

THE SHAPING OF MOUNTAINS

4: NATURE IN THE MOUNTAINS

Life is tough on a mountain. The harsh winter weather with its summer rain, winter snow and deep penetrating frosts, make conditions unbearable for many species. And there are further obstacles to overcome: the air is thin and the slopes steep. So wildlife in the mountains has to be able to resist the winter and be adaptable enough to capitalize on a short summer.

The way plants survive

Plants are the foundation of all food chains, and the plants of the mountains have to be very resilient to survive. There are many ways they succeed in doing this. Some plants hide away among the screes or rocky crevices, using the rocks to protect them from the cold. However, a sheltered site is not always the best, for it is often also a shady site. Many plants, therefore, have to find places that are more exposed to the sun, and of course, to the weather.

The benefits of shelter can be clearly seen in this picture. The plants can thrive between the rocks but they have not succeeded in growing over them.

The lower slopes of all mountains (except those in polar regions) are clothed in forests. Trees may sometimes be found even on desert mountains where the mountains cause relief rain.

The mountain foot supports the same natural pattern of trees and herbs as grow in the surrounding lowlands: in a region near the equator it will be tropical evergreen rainforest; in mid-latitudes it will be deciduous forest; and in higher latitudes it will be conifers. But on all mountains the sequence in which plants are found as they progress up the mountainside are: woody herbs then shrubs followed by conifer. Indeed, for this reason it may be difficult to distinguish one mountain region from another without a close inspection of the species.

Conifers, with their waxy needles, which are both drought and frost resistant, can stand up to harsh weather

Lichens, crust-like plants that cling fast to the surfaces of bare rocks, will survive by extracting their nutrients directly from the rocks they colonize.

Above 3500m. Bogs with giant lobelia, grounsels and lichens.

3000 to 3500m. Giant heather moss forest - mist zone.

2500 to 3000m. Bamboo forest.

1500 to 2500m. Rainforest.

The higher you go up a mountain the lower the air temperature becomes. *Tropical mountains show this excellently. A volcanic mountain like Mount Kenya, for example, rises over 5000 metres above the East African plains.*

At the foot of the mountain there are warm humid conditions that allow rainforest vegetation to thrive. But at higher levels conditions become more difficult and rainforest gives way to a simpler pattern of plants dominated by bamboo. Going higher again, the bamboo limit is reached and above this giant heathers are the only large plant to survive in the cool, foggy air.

At 4000 metres there is frost every night. Not only is the air thin, but it is also dry. Although clouds form on the slopes of the mountain every day, rarely do they grow tall enough to cover the summit. Here the plants have to withstand drought and freezing cold nights.

At the highest levels, the number of plant species is small and growth slow. All plants have to have protection against the cold by producing their own antifreeze. This is the habitat of the extraordinary giant lobelia which stores its antifreeze inside its giant rosette of fleshy leaves.

NATURE IN THE MOUNTAINS 25

better than any other tree. The world's oldest living thing, the bristlecone pine, has lived through over 5000 years of harsh weather in high mountains of western USA. But even conifers cannot live in the highest, coldest and most exposed places. In many places the upper limit of tree growth is surprisingly clear-cut, as though there is some threshold condition that the conifers cannot cope with. Above the 'tree line' are the summit pastures, so called because only grasses, perennial herbs and some dwarf shrubs survive, making summer pasture for herds of wild grazing animals. This is the harsh world called the **tundra**.

Mountain simplicity

Generally speaking, the higher you go up a mountain, the simpler the **ecosystem** becomes. Near the foot there are many species and these can support a wide range of animals, but as environmental conditions become more exacting, not only must animals be able to cope with them, but they also have less variety of plants to feed on.

Cold conditions affect the rate of plant growth and thus the amount of grazing material that is produced each year. And as plant growth slows, so the number of animals it can support also diminishes.

Animals that eat plants are called herbivores. They may be large and agile, like the pronghorn sheep of North America or the vicuna of the Andes in South America, or they may be small, like voles and squirrels. But each in its turn is food for the hunters, or predators – the animals that need to eat meat for food. As the number of herbivores declines, so too, must the number of predators. As a result many of them need to travel over huge areas in order to find enough food. The mountain lion typifies the mobility that such animals must show. The bald eagle and condor are birds with large wingspans, able to glide over their enormous territories with little loss of energy as they seek far and wide for food.

Slow decay

All living things have a certain lifespan. When they die, their bodies become the food for the last part of the ecosystem, the decomposers. Many decomposers, such as

Slow growing and gnarled, conifers are among the most resilient of the mountain plants.

NATURE IN THE MOUNTAINS

bacteria, are very small, but they work by converting dead tissue back into nutrients that living plants can use. The decomposers work much faster in warm than cold conditions. As a result the dead material often only partially breaks down on cold mountains. Peat is a good example. It is the accumulation of partly rotted plant material, and contains pieces of plant that are often many thousands of years old.

When dead plant and animal tissue rots in warm conditions, nutrients are released which act as food for the growing plants.

The alpaca, now domesticated and used in place of sheep in the high Andes in South America, is both agile and able to withstand the chilling winds. The thickness of its coat, which gives much of the protection, is clearly seen in this picture.

But when dead tissue rots slowly and incompletely, a quite different range of products are released. Instead of giving nutrients, the decomposers release acids. Very few plants can tolerate a cold acid soil, and this is a major reason why so few plants grow on many cold mountains.

5: USING THE MOUNTAINS

Traditionally, homes were built out of wood and heated with wood. It was therefore in everyone's interest to ensure the regeneration of the forest.

Self-contained living

Living in areas that were inaccessible, especially when the winter snows blocked the passes, mountain peoples developed their own ways and their own civilizations. The most isolated of all were the peoples of the Himalayas such as the Nepalese and Tibet and the Incas of the South American Andes. The Incas, who controlled a huge mountain empire until the arrival of the Spanish in the sixteenth century, were the most famous of the Andean mountain peoples. Their empire had to be entirely self-contained and

Mountains cause isolation. In the days before cars and aeroplanes, mountains could only be reached after many days of trekking or on horseback. Most people who ventured into mountains only used the passes that allowed them to get to distant lowlands. Isolation has resulted in an enormous diversity of peoples, each adapting to the mountain environment. As generation after generation passed down its knowledge, so people became very sensitive in the ways they managed the environment without destroying it.

The high mountain passes can only be crossed in high summer. In developed countries they have been bypassed using tunnels. In developing countries people still have to wait for the winter snows to melt.

28 USING THE MOUNTAINS

to achieve this they not only built a complex network of routeways, but they discovered many ways of cultivating plants at high altitudes and in the face of frost.

The Incas developed staircases of terraces so that the steep mountainsides could be farmed without losing any of the precious soil. They also devised ways to irrigate their terraces by guiding natural streams onto each terrace bank. But more than this, they were quick to exploit the advantages of nature, cultivating the 150 strains of potato that grew naturally, each in its own special climatic niche.

Machu Picchu, about 80 kilometres northwest of Cuzco, a city in the Peruvian Andes of South America, is one of the most famous ancient cities in the world.

Sitting on top of an eroded volcanic peak, it was built by the Inca people to look over the Urubamba valley. It is about 2 400 metres above sea level and forms an entire town surrounded by agricultural terraces designed to make the town self-sufficient in foodstuffs.

The Inca people had developed a remarkably sophisticated civilization by the fifteenth century, but because they were isolated they shared little with other cultures. For example, the wheel had not been introduced from outside.

Their isolation made them vulnerable to the Spanish conquests of the sixteenth century and their culture was soon destroyed.

USING THE MOUNTAINS

Life goes on much as it has for centuries in these high Himalayan pastures, but the ground now clearly shows the signs of overgrazing and the impact of too many people.

people. So as the numbers of people increase, so do the numbers of animals that are needed to support them. In many places there are now too many families, too many cattle, and too many goats. The land is feeling the strain in several ways.

First the people need wood for fuel to keep warm in the mountains and to cook their food. Trees, however, grow slowly in mountains and their timber is easily exhausted. Furthermore, there are

The Incas even discovered a way of using water to store heat in their fields and make their crops grow faster. They realized that water holds heat better than soil and that a field criss-crossed with waterways can hold the daytime heat better than a dry field.

The Incas were able to learn from nature and so work with the environment for their long-term survival. They had to be sensitive to the soils and the slopes because their livelihoods depended on this.

Feeling the strain

In the developing world many people still live in traditional societies, with many generations living together. But the population has been growing rapidly for several decades and this has added many pressures to their use of the mountains. Cattle, sheep and goats are the main livelihood of most mountain

When people live in a self-sufficient way, their numbers must match the available resources or they will over-use the land. This is what has happened in many mountains, such as here in the Himalayas. These lower mountain slopes were once forested but are so no longer.

USING THE MOUNTAINS

increasing demands for fuelwood from the lowlands, tempting the mountain people to fell trees for money. The resulting loss of forest is called deforestation.

Animals eat the saplings that make the next generation of trees, so with large numbers of animals on the mountains, the forest trees do not get a chance to renew themselves. In addition, people are keen to fell the forests because this gives more room for grass to grow, and thus more grazing land for the animals.

Distant impact

The Himalayas is an example of such pressure and large areas have been denuded of their trees. This is bad for the local environment because the soil is no longer held in place by the tree roots and so it is easily eroded by heavy rains. But perhaps even more important is the way that the rainfall now runs from the mountains more quickly down to the rivers in the valleys below. The tree roots used to make many passageways through the soil, allowing water to sink in and be stored in much the same way as in a sponge. The effect of this natural sponge was that the valleys received the rainwater and snowmelt relatively slowly and so flooding was not common. Today, without trees, water rushes much more quickly to the valleys and flooding is commonplace.

Rivers in flood are powerful agents of erosion and can quickly carry away huge amounts of soil. It is said that today the export of soil by the rivers running from the treeless Himalayas is Nepal's most valuable export – an export Nepal never intended to make.

The swollen, sediment-filled rivers are not welcome in the lowlands because,

The number of animals has increased in proportion to the number of people living in the mountains. Now it is a struggle for each shepherd to find enough grazing land.

as the floodwaters spill out over the land they flood the fields and destroy crops; they lay down a carpet of soil that buries seedlings; and they deposit sediment in the river beds which causes their levels to rise, thus making the chances of future flooding greater still. Now governments of developing countries are trying to think of ways of curbing the ever-growing problems created by farming pressure in the mountains.

The pressure to leave

Mountain people have to be adaptable; the valley bottoms are narrow and the fields that can grow grass and cereals are small. Yet farming in the mountains must often depend on animals because there is so little time for crops to ripen. The solution has traditionally been for people and animals to migrate with the seasons, a system that has come to be known as **transhumance**.

Transhumance starts as the snow leaves the upper slopes above the tree line. Here the high level meadows provide some grazing for animals. And when animals are moved to the high pastures, grazing pressures on the valley bottom pastures is removed and the grass can be allowed to grow to be made into the hay that will be needed for overwintering the animals.

Glaciated valleys provide little scope for farmers. They have to establish their homes in sheltered valley bottom sites, and then look for mountain pastures to use as summer grazing while they use the patchwork of lowland fields to grow fodder for overwintering. This is Solvorn, a village beside a Norwegian fjord.

Cattle grazing on the upland summer pastures. Each has a bell to enable its owner to track it down.

32 USING THE MOUNTAINS

The task of climbing the mountains and living with the animals has traditionally been given to the old people and children. In their summer homes high on the upper shoulders of the valleys, grandparents and grandchildren spend the summer collecting milk from the animals. With no easy means of getting the milk to the valley before the milk goes bad, cheese-making has become a traditional task.

At the end of the summer the animals come down again from the pastures and are housed in sheltered barns, thus completing the cycle of transhumance.

__Winter snow can be so thick__ that whole communities become isolated. If this happens over long periods such homes have to be regarded as summer houses only. Many houses like these in the Italian Alps dot the high pastures and are used only when the cattle and sheep are taken to graze on the highest meadows.

__Forests help to protect valley floor towns__ from the effects of avalanches. But as people forget the traditional skills of maintaining forests, the trees become weak and often do not get replanted. The result is weaker protection for the towns in the valleys below. Adding ski runs on the mountain slopes simply makes the danger worse.

There is pressure on this system of transhumance. In the developed countries children can no longer go to the summer pastures because they are, by law, required to attend school. In any case many young people do not now want to spend the summers isolated from their friends. Developed world farmers can also now import fodder for their animals, and the cost of doing so is subsidized by governments. The result has been that transhumance is largely confined to the developing world. Elsewhere there is much pressure to abandon the mountains.

USING THE MOUNTAINS 33

Many mountain valleys end in steep, high bowl-shaped *corries* that are almost impossible to cross. The villagers that occupy these valleys (such as the one in the picture below) are almost entirely devoted to survival in the mountains. But now such places are ideal quiet spots for second homes (shown right) for those who live in cities. The result has been huge price rises in many mountain villages, rises with which the local people cannot compete. As a result the mix of people is turning away from those who know how to care for the local environment

Water, water

Although mountains may often be unattractive for farming, nearly all of them have one valuable resource in plenty: water. Rain may **leach** soils of their valuable minerals, but if the water can be stored, it can be transported to the lowlands where rainfall is more modest and where the demand is much greater.

Water is used to irrigate lowland crops, to provide hydro-electric power, to be used as a raw material or as cooling water by industry, and to provide people with drinking water. In countries where irrigation is required, agriculture is by far the greatest user of water.

There are many benefits to building dams and creating reservoirs in mountain areas, such as preventing valuable farmland from flooding and generating hydro-electric power. However, large reservoirs do have environmental consequences. The flow of water is regulated for the use of people; this

USING THE MOUNTAINS

is often not good for the wildlife of the rivers. The reservoir levels are drawn down to match demand, often leaving ugly barren ground in summer, at just the time when tourists want to look at the beauty of the mountain landscape, and reservoirs do not contain a balanced ecosystem. Nevertheless, of all the uses of mountains, many would consider that reservoirs are the least damaging.

Hydro-electric power plants are frequently sited in sequences *to make the best use of the water resources. In this picture you can see pipes leading water from a high level lake to the turbines housed by the lakeside. The water is then released into the lake and later fed to a power plant lower down the valley.*

Getting about

Isolation has been one of the main reasons why so little has altered in mountain environments. But change comes quickly when access is improved. And so it has been with the mountains of many developed countries. Just a few years ago the only way through mountains was by pack donkey. The electric train altered that, by making once remote areas easy for anyone to get to. Goods could now be brought in and taken from mountain regions. Since then roads and even motorways have improved access even more dramatically. This has opened up a whole new range of possible uses for mountains besides farming, forestry and water supply.

USING THE MOUNTAINS

Mountain pressures have been changed dramatically by the introduction of better communications. Below is a Swiss rack and pinion railway, the first mode of transport to change accessibility in the mountains. On the right is a picture of snow-clearing machine removing the last snow from a road on a high pass. However, most major mountain routes are open all year through the use of tunnels.

Riches in the ground

Traditional farming methods enabled people to make a living without disturbing the soils much. But fertile soil is not the only wealth of the mountains. Many also contain precious minerals such as gold, silver and copper, and the prospect of great wealth has attracted quite a different group of people – those who, in general have no knowledge of, or sympathy for, the mountain environment.

Some of the most famous mountain prospecting has been in America. There have been famous strikes of gold and silver all over the mountains, some starting a veritable stampede of people, such as in the Californian 'Gold Rush' of 1849.

Most small-scale miners use primitive tools and primitive methods. They hack at the soil and discard it, then hack at the rock and discard most of this too. They divert streams to wash the rock from the mineral and then let the sediment-filled stream flow where they please. Eventually,

USING THE MOUNTAINS

when the mineral is exhausted they simply move to somewhere new, leaving the mountain land to recover the best way it can. This is still the method used by peasant miners all over the developing world.

Modern mechanized mining is different. Whether operated in the mountains of Colorado, USA or Papua New Guinea, it is not primitive and it is not hit and miss. But it is also far more destructive of the environment because modern methods can extract minerals from ores that would be impossible by traditional techniques. The new prospectors can extract minerals with a concentration of just a few grammes of mineral in a tonne of rock. To make economic sense of such mining whole mountains are destroyed. It is truly landscape forming on a grand scale.

Many mountains contain large mineral resources, but when the mines are no longer economic, they were abandoned without any thought of covering the industrial scars.

These pictures show two typical forms of mining near Leadville, Colorado, USA. Here the town was named after a mineral strike. Lead is very poisonous and the waste (called tailings) remains uncolonized by vegetation many decades after the mines were abandoned.. The bottom picture shows the terrible state of the land from early mining.

The top picture shows the modern mine nearby. To get to the mineral (in this case a metal called molybdenum which is used to make special steels) the mountain was blasted away and a huge quarry as well as underground tunnels created. This mine, too, has now been closed because it is uneconomic. It is too early to say whether or not it will be re-opened and how the scars will be dealt with if the mine remains closed.

USING THE MOUNTAINS

The tools for a successfully developed piste. *In the foreground is the ski lift that takes people effortlessly to the top of the piste. Behind it is the machine that smooths out the piste as it becomes worn and rutted through heavy ski use. It can trundle up even very steep pistes to clear the ground using its weight to help compact the snow. Such machines have a severe impact on the ground beneath the snow.*

On the tourist trail

Today life in many mountain regions has changed dramatically. Old routeways and narrow twisting roads have been replaced by broad, well-graded roads, and even motorways. But it is not the needs of the farmers or the miners that have caused such efforts to be made. Rather, it is the arrival of the very people who, two centuries ago, shunned the mountains as horrible and forbidding places – the tourists.

Tourists visit the mountains throughout the year. In winter, where the land is suitable, the main form of tourism is skiing. Skiing is a very concentrated form of tourism and it places enormous demands on the environment, demands of which the skiers are often unaware.

Winter cross country *skiing can compact the ground below.*

USING THE MOUNTAINS

A skiing trail (a piste) is mostly a creation of the skiing industry, rarely is it a natural phenomenon. Trees have to be cut down to provide fast yet safe tracks; machines have to be used to grade and regrade the ice as it gets worn and rutted by skis; and chair and cable lifts have to be provided to get the skiers to the top of the pistes.

With thousands of skiers using the same areas of land, the pressure on the vegetation and soil is harsh, even though there may seem to be a protective cover of snow. But the skiers also demand access to their resorts: hotels, car parks, trains, restaurants, and much more.

A resort that only operates for part of the year makes less sense than one which can be open all year round. So the hotel owners are keen to attract summer tourists for walking and sightseeing holidays. Many mountains are criss-crossed with walking routes, which are easily eroded under the high amount of foot pressure.

But with the tourists come the cars and the coaches bringing pollution. They add to the concentration of harmful gases like **ozone** near the ground, and they add to the effect of **acid rain** in the air. Mountain lands, with their thin, heavily leached soils find it hard to resist the extra pollution pressure. Many are dying, more will surely go.

Skiing places great demands on the landscape. *This slope shows all the signs of change due to heavy skiing. While a few trees make interesting markers for skiers to zig-zag round, many trees either slow skiers down and make the piste uninteresting, or they present too much of an obstacle and are dangerous. As a result, there is great pressure to remove trees from areas near ski resorts.*

The land after the spring thaw *shows clearly how the forest has been cut to make skiing trails. Notice the eroded areas where skiers drag their skis while moving along the lift routes.*

USING THE MOUNTAINS

6: IS THERE A FUTURE?

We can only care for our environments if we understand how they work, and appreciate the reasons why they are threatened. For example, we cannot just worry about the numbers of tourists in an area and how to make the roads wide enough to accommodate them. We have to understand the impact of the roads on the way water moves through the soil, and on the way roads and traffic might interfere with the natural wildlife by frightening it away, removing its habitat or through the effects of exhaust pollution.

In this book we have seen that rugged mountains support a finely balanced ecosystem. Caring for the environment means making sure the whole ecosystem survives, not just parts of it. Mountains have simple patterns of life that are already under stress from the cold climate. Adding trampling feet and pollution may push many lands beyond their ability to recover.

Traditional ways

As mountainous areas become more populated, the pressure will increase. In the past traditional people were good guardians of the mountain environment, but today in the developing world the number of people are overtaxing the land's resources and they may actually destroy the land they love.

These people do not destroy their land willingly, but they see no choice if they are to survive. To prevent further destruction, people have to be made to see the dangers for themselves and they have to be shown the means to improve their land in new ways, but with respect for the traditions of the people and their needs.

Mountains can be made more productive, can still be farmed traditionally and soil loss can be halted. This new understanding has been introduced recently in Nepal, where the soil is being eroded more quickly than anywhere else on Earth.

The future relies on restoring the ecosystem to a better balance. Quick

Farmers should be encouraged, *even subsidized, to stay on their land and farm it in traditional ways. Mountain meadows, for example, provide the opportunities for many species to thrive as well as giving fodder for animals. This is a meadow carpeted with crocuses in spring.*

IS THERE A FUTURE?

Getting about in mountains *has traditionally been difficult. Leaving some roads undeveloped will restrict the number of tourists and relieve these areas of excessive pressure.*

growing conifer trees can be planted on eroded land to stabilize it. With larger numbers of trees, the runoff from the heavy rains will produce less damaging floods in the lowlands and keep the soil where it should be, on the mountains!

Many species of broad-leaved trees, for example birches, grow naturally among the conifers. Within a few years the conifers can be harvested for fuelwood and a broadleaved forest will remain to protect the soil. Below the trees, grass will grow that can be fed to cattle.

Farmers now see that they can get more from the land and still protect it. The methods fit in with the natural lifestyle of the people and the future is more secure.

Modern mountain motorways can be a good thing *for mountains if they take the pressure off the valleys and focus people on the resorts. It means that more effort can be put into caring for the smaller number of more heavily used areas.*

IS THERE A FUTURE?

Some areas of mountain should be protected by National Parks so that there will be no disturbance to the natural habitat, so that it can survive. However, such parks have to be very large because mountains offer only limited food for the carnivores that live there, and they must range widely to find their prey.

Keeping reserves

It is vital to preserve some areas as wilderness before they are put under development pressure. A country such as Bhutan in the Himalayas is an ideal region to begin a scheme of National Parks because it does not yet have a large population. In the developed world some National Parks have been in existence for nearly 100 years. Foremost among these are the parks of the USA and Canada, areas that are large enough to allow the wildlife to live in a natural balance.

As more and more people seek recreation, the siting of new resorts becomes very important if some areas are to remain untouched.

IS THERE A FUTURE?

National Parks preserve the wilderness and give wildlife a future. But they also do much more. By organizing the parks for visitors they can show people why the wilderness is worth preserving and the ways this can be achieved. In developed countries people still have the choice of how to use the land. The more people who understand the value of wilderness, the easier it will be to find the money and support to preserve more land.

Caring for the mountain environments must start thousands of kilometres away in the lowland industrial zones. The amount of sulphur and nitrogen oxides produced here falls on the mountain forests with often devastating effects.

A global challenge

Mountains may seem far from where most people live, but, with today's technology, they are not as isolated as many people think. The pollution created in the industrial areas is swiftly carried to all parts of the globe, and when it reaches fragile areas like mountains, the wildlife is particularly hard hit.

We cannot hope to leave a future of healthy mountain wildlife if we pollute the land so badly it cannot recover. The future of the mountains, depends, as much as anything, on controlling the way we live in the lowlands throughout the world.

IS THERE A FUTURE?

GLOSSARY

acid rain
rain which has significant amounts of sulphur and nitrogen gases dissolved in it, making the rain much more acid than it would naturally be

corrie
bowl-shaped hollows in mountainsides that have been formed by the scouring action of small glaciers

crust
the surface layers of the Earth that are made of cool, quite solid and brittle rocks

ecosystem
a balanced arrangement of plants, animals, soil and climate. An ecosystem is a stable unit, with the decay of dead organisms providing the food for those that are growing

fold mountain
a mountain that has been formed from sedimentary rocks that have been crushed up by the collision of the Earth's crust during continental drift

Ice Age
a period when the world's ice sheets expanded greatly. As a result many areas lost their natural vegetation and it has only just recovered

leach
the chemical process of dissolving nutrients in a soil and carrying them out of the root zones with percolating rainwater

mantle
the region of the Earth below the crust containing regions that are plastic and which can move very slowly, perhaps a few centimetres a year. Movements within the mantle cause plates to move

ozone
a form of oxygen that absorbs harmful ultra-violet radiation from the Sun. The ozone layer acts like a shield in the outer parts of our atmosphere

plates
the name given to large pieces of the crust that move across the Earth's surface under the drag from movements within the mantle

rainshadow
an area which lies behind a large mountain range which blocks off the flow of moist, rain-bearing winds. As a result rainshadow areas get a reduced rainfall

screes
piles of loose rocks that have fallen and accumulated at the foot of a steep slope. They are typically produced as the result of frost shatter in mountain regions

sediment
the material carried by a river. The finest sediment is called clay and this is responsible for muddying floodwaters. Larger sizes of sediment are called silt, sand, gravel, pebbles and boulders respectively

transhumance
the practice of moving between valley and mountain shoulder to take advantage of the summer pastures that occur at high levels

tundra
a treeless region which experiences cold climates throughout the majority of the year and where the average annual temperature is below freezing

INDEX

acid rain 39, 44
Alps 12, 18
Andes 11, 18, 28
animals 30
Appalachians 18
ash 20
Asia 11
atmosphere 14

barrier 9
Britain 18

civilization 28
cloud 14
conifer 24, 41
continental drift 18
copper 12, 36
corrie 34, 44
crust 18, 44

dam 34
decomposer 26
deforestation 31

earthquake 20
ecosystem 26, 40, 44
environment 30
erosion 13, 20
eruption 21

farming 9, 36, 40, 41
fertile 20
flood 34, 41
flood plain 23
fog 17
fold mountain 18, 44
forest 24, 31
fracture 19
frost 16, 24

glacier 8, 22
gold 9, 36

granite 20
grazing 31, 32
ground moraine 23

habitat 40
herbivore 26
Himalayas 11, 16, 18, 28, 31, 42
hydro-electric power 34

ice 18
Ice Age 22, 44
Indonesia 10, 20
interlocking spur 23
irrigate 29, 34
island arc 20

Japan 10, 20

lake 23
lava 19
leach 34, 39, 44
leeward 12, 14
limestone 20

mantle 19, 44
migrate 32
minerals 12, 34
miners 36
moisture 16
motorway 35, 38
Mount Everest 8, 18

National Parks 42

ocean 18
ozone 39, 44

Pacific Ocean 11
pass 28
pasture 26
peat 27

piste 39
plate 18, 44
pollution 39, 40
population 30
predator 26
prospecting 36

quarrying 22

rain 14, 18, 24, 31
rainshadow 16, 44
relief rain 16, 24
reservoir 34
resort 39
river 23
Rocky Mountains 11, 18

Scandinavia 18
scree 23, 44
sediment 18, 31, 36, 44
silver 9, 36
skiing 12, 38
snow 14, 18, 24, 28
soil 31

terrace 29
till 23
timber 30
tourist 38, 40
transhumance 32, 44
tree line 26
tundra 26, 44

volcano 11, 20

water 34
waterfall 23
weather 9, 12, 14
wilderness 42
wildlife 24, 40
wind 16
windward 12, 14

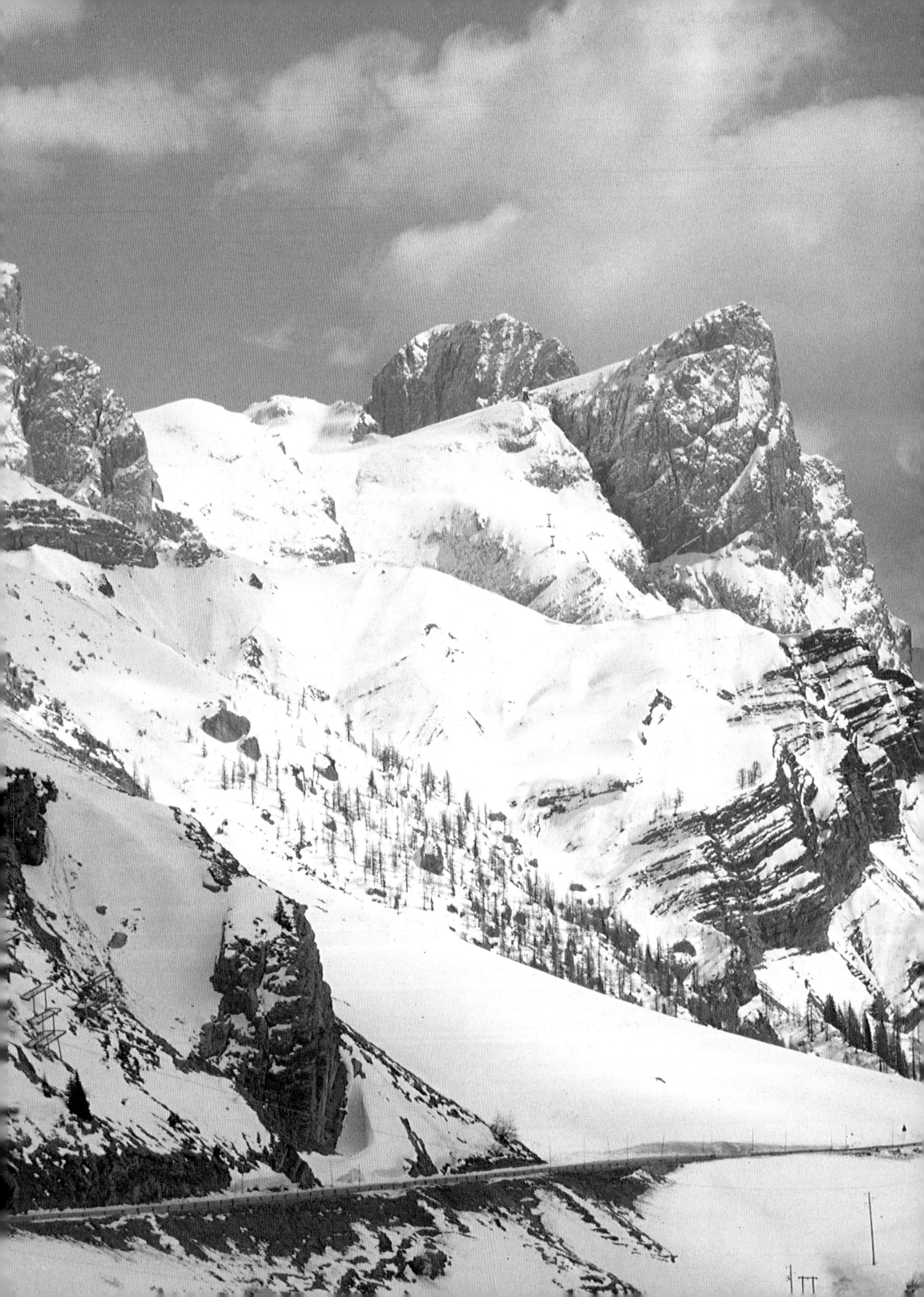